If you have purchased this book without its cover, it may be a stolen book. Neither the publisher or the author is under any obligation to provide professional services in anyway, legal, health or in any form which is related to this book, its contents advice or otherwise.

The law and practices vary from country to country and state to state. If legal or professional information is required, the purchaser, or the reader should seek the information privately and best suited to their particular needs and circumstances.

The author and the publisher specifically disclaim any liability that may be incurred from the information within this book.

All rights reserved.

No part of this book, including the interior design, images cover design, diagrams, or any intellectual property (IP), icons and photographs may be reproduced or transmitted in any form by any means (electronic, photocopying, recording or otherwise) without the prior permission of the publisher.

ISBN: 978-0-6480836-5-8

Copyright© 2018 MSI Australia
All rights reserved.

Published by Books For Reading On Line.com .,
under licence from MSI Ltd, Australia
Company Registration No: 96963518255
NSW, Australia

This book forms part of the CPD Accredited Course for Fast Track Commercial Floristry Course

See our website: www.how-to-books.com & www.booksforreadingonline.com

Or contact by email: sales@booksforreadingonline.com or: admin@booksforreadingonline.com
Front & Back Covers and Copyright owned by MSI, Australia

MSI acknowledges the author of the images used in this book.

Photography by Christine Thompson-Wells ©
How-To-Books.com is a subsidiary of Books For Reading On Line.com

Welcome to this book of

How to Create

Easy Flower Arrangements

In the following pages you will be given step-by-step direction on how to create a number of different floral arrangements.

You will gain information about colour, texture, shape, form, placement and the principles of design and art in floral arranging.

The journey of learning about flowers and deeply looking at the flower as an individual creation of beauty is a good way to reduce stress while learning new creative skills.

Flowers have been used for many thousands of years for celebrations, offerings and to help people express their emotions. The flowers we use today have been in creation and evolution for millions of years; as you work with these creations, please give respect to the treasures and gifts you are working with.

As a trained florist and educator, I can say with all my heart, '…to create a beautiful piece of floral art is a personal journey; it gives me great personal rewards and satisfaction'.

About The Author

Christine Thompson-Wells trained as a florist in London.

She has owned and run many successful florist shop businesses and taught many students in her own floristry school and taught floral design, art, visual merchandising and many other subjects at the Canberra Institute of Technology and is a Further Education teacher.

Christine, because of the need for florists to enter the workforce, initiated the commercial floristry course in 1984 at Canberra Institute of Technology where the course is still running at Bruce Campus, Bruce, Canberra in the Australian Capital, Australia.

She says, 'the course took four long years to bring to fruition but, thankfully, it's still running in 2017.'

After selling one of her businesses, Christine was appointed as the florist for the Prime Minister and Mrs Fraser at the Prime Minister's Lodge, Canberra, Australia. During that time she created the floral arrangements for one of the Queen's visits to Australia; she has been a writer for Flora International where her work was published to a worldwide audience.

Feeling the need to know more, after selling one of the businesses, Christine went to university to study Education and Psychology. She says, 'the reason I went to university was that I wanted to know why people bought flowers?' This question has led her on to do a great deal of writing and has had many books and articles published on the study of human behaviour. She writes within a large genre which includes: children's books, books on mind health and wellbeing, poetry and a range of other subjects.

Content	Page
❖ *To Begin*	1
❖ The Tools You Will Need	2
❖ Understanding Design	3
❖ Colour	4
❖ Texture	5
❖ Choosing Simple Containers	6
❖ Flower Designs: Starting At The Beginning –	
❖ Traditional Vertical Arrangement	7
❖ Traditional Horizontal Flower Arrangement	9
❖ Traditional 'Fan-Shaped' (Bilateral) Flower Arrangement	12
❖ Traditional Posy Bowl Flower Arrangement	15
❖ Traditional Crescent Shape Flower Arrangement	18
❖ Loose-Cut, Layered, Two-Colour Flower Arrangement	21
❖ A Variation On A Two-Colour Flower Arrangement	23
❖ A Traditional, Loose Australian Native Flower Arrangement Using Layered, Colours In Fruit	25
❖ Taking A Different Slant On Fruit And Flower Arrangements	27
❖ A Simple Box Of Flowers	30
❖ A Two-Flower Arrangement	32
❖ Pretty In Pinks	34
❖ A Combination Of Three	37
❖ How Pretty Are Blue And Pink?	39
❖ Making Easy Christmas Arrangements	41
❖ A Christmas Treat	43

To Begin

With any flower arrangement you create, you will need to have an idea of your design in your mind.

Many people begin to make a flower arrangement and don't realise that pre-planned, mental thinking is the key to great design work. Yes, you can be lucky and sometimes without any pre-planning the design works but that may be a rare occasion. In many instances, unplanned flower arranging can become a very costly experience in the loss of flowers, foliage, money and time.

In order for you to enjoy your flower arranging, I'm now going to take you on a prescribed and easy journey to create beautiful, easy flower arrangements.

To make the arrangements easier to create, you will use simple containers and containers best suited to the items you have available or to the items which are cost effective to you.

Simple Tips

1. With each placement (stem end) put into the oasis, think before the end is inserted. By doing this, you will stay in control of your design.

2. Choose your flowers and foliage with discretion and think about their placements within your design before either first cutting or buying.

3. Study the location of your flower arrangement and ask:
    a. Do the colours fit the surrounding and
    b. Are the flowers I'm using fitting for the occasion?

4. Do not cross the stems of your flowers when inserting them into the oasis. Crossing of stem ends in oasis leads to the oasis becoming weak and will not support your design if the design is a large piece of work.

5. Know that rotting foliage in the oasis shortens the life of your flowers and the beauty of your design.

6. Pre-mental planning leads to beautifully created designs.

The Tools You Will Need

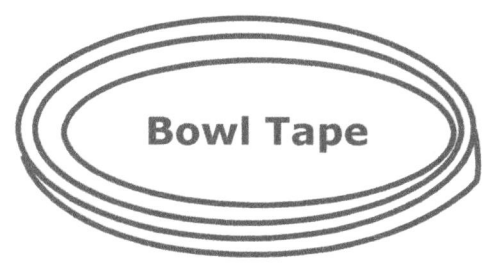

Bowl Tape

Only use bowl tape if you are concerned about the security of your arrangement. Bowl tape can interfere with your placements as you put the stem ends into the oasis.

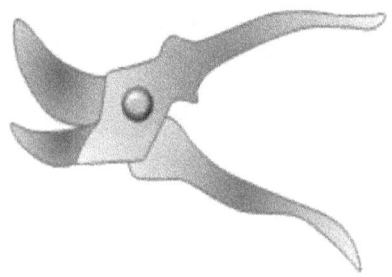

Secateurs

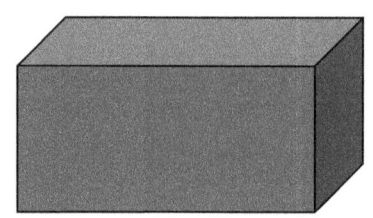

Oasis

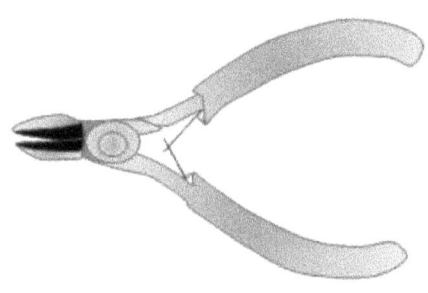

Wire Cutters

Scissors

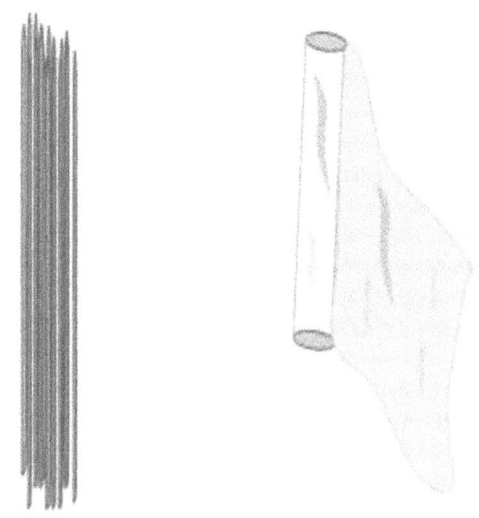

Wooden Skewers and Cling Film.

Understanding Design

Flower design and arranging have some basic principles in construction.

When I trained as a florist, the one thing that was taught to the Nth degree, was 'proportion, rhythm and scale in design'.

The floral artist's aim is to design artistic and beautiful designs in flowers, foliage, vines and other collected or found materials.

There must be an understanding of some basic guidelines before a beautiful design can be created. The Golden Section (please see below) will help you to evaluate and proportion the size and shape of the container to the material you will be using. It will also help you to understand about height, width and the space to leave with the placements of flowers or foliage that you make.

The understanding of proportion is foremost and is an integral part of creativity, regardless of the size and creation being undertaken. Understanding proportion is equally as important as knowing about texture, colour and pattern in design.

The Gold Section

1. Draw 10 inch (25.4cm) line

   _____

2. Divide the line into 2 equal sections

   _____|_____

3. Divide the line into 4 equal sections.

   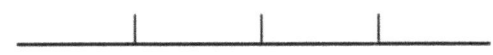

4. Divide the line into 8 equal sections.

   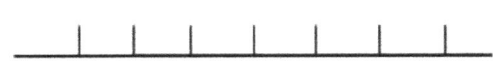

5. Separate into sections of 3 and 5

   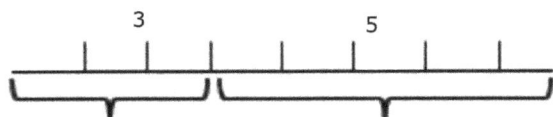

The Golden Section is based roughly on a ratio of 2 to 3; this is a natural mathematical progression and works equally in flower design as to other areas of proportion and scale within all forms of art or artistic creations including architecture.

For example: 2 : 3 = 5; 3 : 5 = 8; 5 : 8 = 13 and so on. These proportions give visual balance. This method of proportion was well known and used by the ancient Greeks. The Golden Section allows the balance of one unit to another, this giving proportion to the amount of area allowed in the whole arrangement or creation.

Colour

For true colour to be seen it needs light. Colour has an emotional appeal which plays on our senses.

Colours are broken down as seen in the diagrams shown on this page.

1)

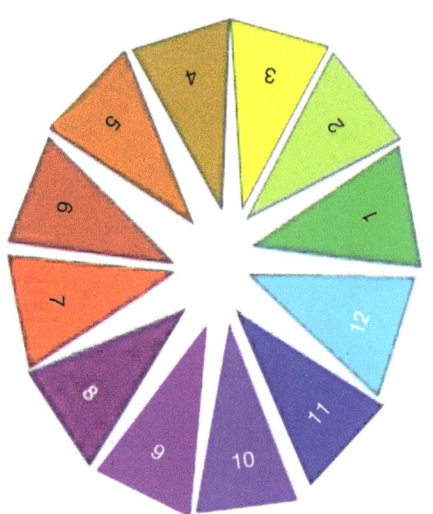

1 Green
2 Yellow-Green
3 Yellow
4 Yellow-Orange
5 Orange
6 Red-Orange
7 Red
8 Red-Violet
9 Violet
10 Blue-Violet
11 Blue
12 Blue-Green

2) **Primary Colours**

Red

Yellow

Blue

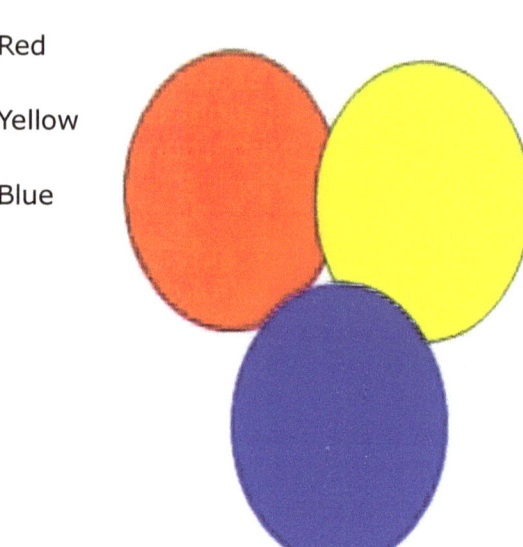

3) **Primary and Secondary Colours**

Red

Yellow

Blue

Secondary Colours:

Green

Violet

Orange

Texture

Like colour, texture does have expressive qualities. Surprisingly, there are both masculine and feminine qualities in texture. The masculine quality is seen in bark, knitting, hessian cloth, the petals of disbud chrysanthemum flowers, in many Australian native flowers and foliages and in other course or rugged surfaces.

Feminine texture is seen in the surface of chiffon, the surface of rose petals, on the petals of spring blossoms and other surfaces that are smooth to the touch or to the eye.

Understanding how texture works in flower arrangements and floral design is critical as texture can either add or take away, not only the visual balance, but also the appeal of your creation.

When talking about texture, we describe it as:

- Smooth
- Fine
- Medium
- Course and
- Rough

Large elements on the surface of the plant or flower will produce course texture and small elements will produce fine texture.

Your eyes will move slowly over course texture and rapidly over fine texture. If you like course or rough textures such as looking a bark, it creates in your mind a sense of slowness – stoppage points for the eyes to rest upon. When you look at a smooth texture, the smooth texture creates a visual sense of speed and allows your mind to be alert and clear.

If texture is an overpowering element, it can destroy what may have otherwise been a very good floral design. One of the obstacles to overcome in floral design is to understand the proportion of texture to colour. For example, when using white or light-coloured gerberas in a design a problem often arises. Gerberas are strong in texture but may be light in colour. I suggest the container should be strong in appearance but not necessarily in colour and a strong foliage such as a broad-leafed, light in colour, Australian gum foliage can be used to balance and to give visual appeal to the floral arrangement.

To give you some idea of the visual misleading messages texture can give to your visual senses, think of a single bird's feather. The texture of the feather is medium or course but appeals to our sense of touch. We know in our mind the softness and weight of the feather, therefore, the texture is misleading.

Choosing Simple Containers

To keep the directions simple, choose a simple, free-standing vase. For most of the designs I'm going to speak about; I'm using a wide tumbler shaped container.

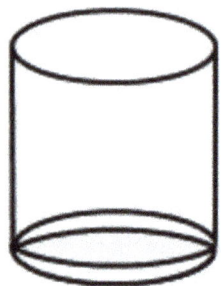

I'm going to line the tumbler with wide green leaves facing outwards. By doing this, I keep the cost of buying expensive vases down, but I can also use different inserts from colourful leaves to water resistant ribbon.

Place a piece of oasis, a little smaller than the size of the container, then soak well prior to inserting into your container. Make sure the oasis sits slightly higher than the container rim.

Fill your container with water before you start placing your foliage and flowers into the oasis.

Before you start arranging any floral arrangement, make sure your flowers and foliage are well conditioned by having a good drink and they are ready in a bucket of water next to your container.

Hot Tip
Containers should not be expensive, candle holders, now readily available with many candles sold, make excellent vases.

Flower Designs: Starting At The Beginning

Traditional Vertical Flower Arrangement

Flowers and foliage used in this arrangement:

- 2 varieties of small-leafed foliage
- 14 small roses, if roses aren't available substitute with: small chrysanthemums, tulips or other small single-stemmed flowers.

With your flowers, foliage and tools in place, you can start to create your design.

The first placement measures one and one half the times the height of the container. If, for instance, your container measures 15cm or 6 inches, your first cut measurement: – flower or foliage, should be about: 38cm or 15 inches tall. Allow about 2.5cm or 1 inch of extra stem to penetrate into the oasis.

The first placement (a) is inserted into the oasis at least two-thirds from the front of the oasis and container. By doing this, you are giving yourself enough space on the oasis to insert the next stems. Always keep in mind where you are inserting the stem end when placing into the oasis.

This first arrangement is a 90 degree arrangement and is a basic design.

The first placement is the vertical placement and establishes the height of your arrangement. Your second and

a

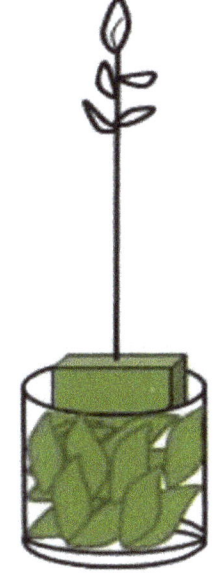

b

third placements (b) are in the horizontal placements and establish the width of your arrangement.

Mastering the simple technique of controlling your placements as you learn how to arrange flowers will save you time, effort, money and stress...

The foundation you work on in any floral design is fundamental to creating good floral arrangements.

Follow the steps:

1. You can see the first, second and third placements with the foliage ends inserted into the oasis. More foliage is added to create a framework before you start to add your flowers.
2. The first, second and third roses are added. I place different textured foliage into the oasis to create a contrast as I place my flowers into the design.
3. More roses are added. Each flower added should be at a slightly different level and angle when placed into the oasis. By doing this you keep the visual rhythm of the flowers moving which adds pleasure to your eye.
4. More roses are added to the design giving depth and appeal.
5. The focal area in any design is where the eye rests. In the picture opposite, the focal area is where the larger roses are placed at slightly different angles in the lower part of the design; extra interest is added by grouping of bunches of red berries.

Hot Tip
Create your design in your mind before you start to create your arrangement in real flowers.

Traditional Horizontal Flower Arrangement

Flowers and foliage used in this arrangement:

- 15 small roses
- Nandina and mixed foliage.

The previous design was ninety degrees – straight up and down. The horizontal design is the same line as looking at a table top or any flat, straight line surface.

Using the same container as before, the placements will go in a straight line horizontally.

Because you are learning traditional line design, the first measurements are the same for both the vertical and horizontal arrangements:

a. Your container is ready with the oasis in place.
b. The first placement is a light piece of foliage placed at one side of the oasis.
c. The overall measurement of your arrangement will be: 38cm or 15 inches in the horizontal measurement. For the horizontal design, divide this measurement into three. On one side of the oasis your first placement will be: 10 inches, or about 25.5cm (allow for the stem end that goes into the oasis). The second placement will measure 5 inches or about 12.5cm in length, again allow enough stem end to go into the oasis. Once you are happy with the first two placements, follow the next diagram.
d. Small-leafed foliage is cut shorter than the measurements of your established first placements.

a

b
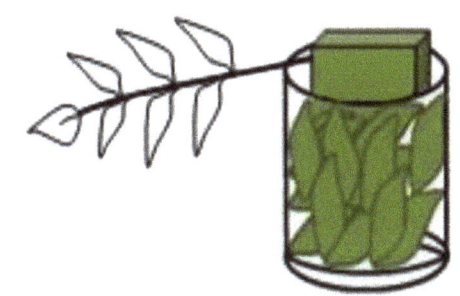

c

d

Follow the steps:

1. In picture 1, you can see a variety of masculine and feminine textured foliages are used as transition materials within the established horizontal shape of the design.
2. 3 roses are used as the first flower placements. These first placements are the complete overall measurement of the first placement, please re-read item (c) in the above.
3. More roses are added showing the overall line of the design.
4. Strength is added to the design by more rose placements being singly measured and then cut to the required measurement within the design.
5. The completed design with roses and small red berries added to the focal area giving a point of interest within the overall arrangement.

Many beautiful designs can be made with very few flowers. It is however the way you work with your mind that will determine the success of your creations.

5

Hot Tip
In many instances, your flowers will dictate the design you create. The secret of great designs: make the very best out of the materials you have available.

Traditional 'Fan Shaped' (Bilateral) Flower Arrangement

Flowers and foliage used in this arrangement:

- Various small-leafed foliage
- 6 small white spray carnations with buds
- 7 salmon-coloured roses
- 8 yellow roses and
- Small white narcissus flowers.

Bilateral symmetry design simply means a two-sided, equally proportioned and visually balanced floral arrangement. Because the flowers placed into the arrangement appear to be balanced – *balance only comes about through careful and thoughtful placements.*

Many outstanding designs have beautiful balance; visual balance comes through flowers being placed at different heights, size, colour and texture throughout the design.

This type of balance takes careful choice of flower types and shapes and the foliage placed within the design which aids to the transition, from one element to another in flower or leaf placements as you create your design.

With the bilateral traditional design, your first placements similar to the first designs you have created:

a. Determine the length of your first placement within the vertical placement with your flowers or foliage. Please refer to the vertical

a

b

c

and horizontal arrangements you have previously created.

b. Establish the length of your horizontal placements then create a fan-shape in your design – this shape is the establishment of your arrangement's shape.
c. Once the vertical and horizontal placements are in place, fill in the shape as shown in the diagram (c). NB: Do not make your placements longer than your established vertical or horizontal placements. The first rose placements are seen in this diagram.

The pictures opposite show how the arrangement develops in shape, form and colour within the materials being used.

Follow the steps:

1. The overall shape of the bilateral symmetry design is determined by the shape you create with the foliage you use.
2. Once the foliage placements are established, the first placement is a small white spray carnation flower followed by a second white carnation flower and then the orange rose.
3. More orange roses and small white jonquil flowers are now established as part of the arrangement's framework.
4. As I create the design, I work with the way I'm thinking. I know from the choices I have made that the flowers will lead to the future placements I will make. Beautiful flow and movement can be created by creating blocks of colour or texture within your work. In this design, the yellow roses are acting as a visual counter-balance in the overall design.

1

2

3

5   The completed design showing grace and movement between the flower shapes, foliage texture and the combination of the colours used.

4

5

Hot Tip
Many combinations of colour can be used in flower arrangement and design, however, by using just three colours you will keep your designs looking tasteful and elegant.

Traditional Posy Bowl Flower Arrangement

Flowers and foliage used in this arrangement:

- 10 yellow roses
- 2 stems of yellow spray chrysanthemums
- A variety of small-leafed foliage

A posy bowl arrangement is not a simple design to create but it can be one of the most admired.

Use the same container as in the first three arrangements this will give you continuity in the learning you are doing. First, measure your first placement, again using the measurement of one and one half times the height of the container. With the second placements, which are the horizontal placements, take the one and a half times, in this instance, its 15 inches (38cm) divide this measurement in two which gives you 7.5 inches or (19cm around the oasis).

In the diagrams opposite:

a. The first measurements are seen placed into the oasis.
b. A bird's eye view of your arrangement. Different pieces of foliage are cut to the required length and inserted into the side of the oasis. For security and to allow the foliage enough moisture push stem ends in about 1 inch (2.5cm) of stem to penetrate the oasis.
c. The profile of the posy bowl arrangements shows how the flower stem sits in the centre of the oasis.
d. The profile of the arrangement showing how the design is created.

a

b
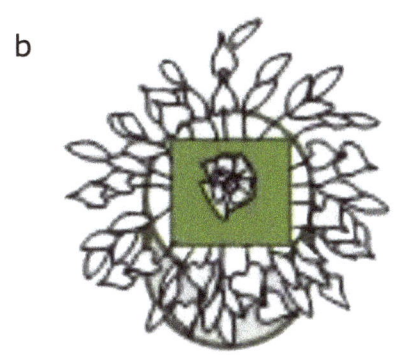

c
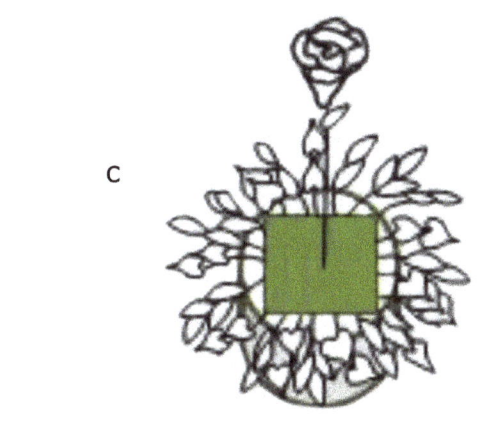

d
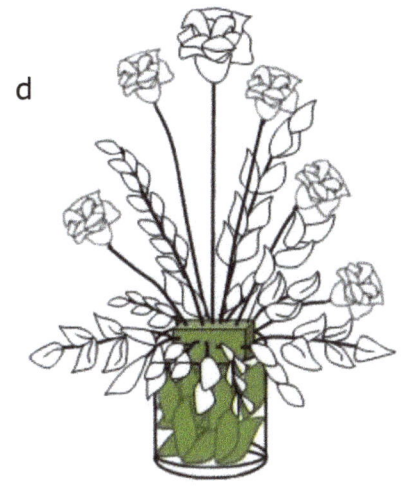

A good sense of proportion and control over your material can be achieved by rotating the container as you place your flowers and foliage into the arrangement.

Follow the steps:

1. The stem ends with the finer leaves of red and green Nandina foliage are inserted evenly around the edge of the oasis.
2. A single yellow rose stem is measured to the correct measurement, cut and inserted into the middle of the oasis.
3. A further 4 placements of yellow roses and chrysanthemums are measured, cut and placed and the sides of the oasis.
4. A second, vertical placement by a chrysanthemum is made and can be seen in this picture.
5. More flowers are added into the design and are worked within your first established framework of leaves and flowers.
6. The completed design can be seen from many angles. Such a design can be made for the boudoir, or on a grand scale, can be the centre piece in the foyer of an impressive building.

By using the techniques spoken of in this arrangement, the design can be made with an impressive modern slant using Phalaenopsis orchids, tropical leaves and spear grass.

Hot Tip
If you want to make a large arrangement using the posy bowl technique, keep in mind your location, availability of flowers and plant material, and importantly: the type of container available. Do not make your ideas impossible to achieve!

4

5

6

Traditional Crescent Shape Flower Arrangement

Flowers and foliage used in this arrangement:

- Budding spring branches
- 17 small red roses
- 2 stems of red Tiger lily
- Small-leafed foliage

To start to create this design you will need to think carefully about the first stem end placements you put in the oasis, please see (a). Unlike many conventional arrangements, working with this design the first placement is still 2/3rds from the front of the oasis and the first stem end penetrates into the centre of the oasis as shown in this diagram.

The second placement (b); the stem end is inserted into the oasis slightly to the left of the first placement.

The third placement (c) is inserted into the oasis at the right side of the first and second placements. A flower is then measured, cut and placed into the oasis to the left side of the second placement. This is a demanding design and will take a lot of concentration to achieve a beautiful piece of work.

Follow the steps:

1. Measure your first placement at least one and one half times the height of the container. In this placement, you will use the same measurements as in the previous four arrangements. Then cut a second, shorter piece of budding spring branch or equivalent and place next to your first placement.
2. Measure, cut and insert placements 3 and 4.

a

b

c

3. Carefully think about your next placements. Try to work with stems that have a natural curve in them. By doing this, your arrangement has a natural flow to its appeal.
4. You will see by the picture that 6 red roses are in place. When choosing the roses to put into the correct placement in your design, look for the size of the rose head, the shape of the stem and how it will fit within your overall design?
5. Using Tiger lily flowers can prove to be cost effective. Choose Tiger lilies that have a long stem from the flower base to the stem crown. If you are buying your flowers, by knowing this, you can save yourself money. The first of the lily bud flower stem's is inserted into the oasis and into its place within the design. Extra roses have been visually measured, cut and placed into the design.
6. The completed design with the focal area shown. Opening lilies will provide days of satisfaction as their beauty unfurls. The colours in a one-colour arrangement can be tantalizing to the eye – they literally become a study during their short life.

Discipline, concentration, the study of the materials you want to use are all connected to the flower arrangement you want to make. Being confident in creating flower arrangements can take many years of practice, thinking about and anticipation. You may think: 'what if?' 'how would that look?' 'perhaps?' Each flower arrangement you create is a jigsaw puzzle to make so please think carefully before you start your design.

Hot Tip
Always well condition (leave all material in water drinking (for hours if necessary or overnight) before you start to create your design.

1

2

3

4

5

6

Loose-Cut, Layered, Two-Colour Flower Arrangement

Choosing A Simple Container

I am using a glass, diamond shaped container for this arrangement. The container measures 8 inches or 20cm. The water in the container comes to half of the measurement of the container. In this instance 4 inches or 10cm.

Flowers and foliage used in this arrangement:

- 10 pink tulips
- 6 stems of blue hyacinths

Follow the diagrams from 1 – 6. The X on the diagrams shows the point at which to keep all of the tulip stems straight and acts as your central stem connection point.

Makes sure the flowers are all cut to the same length. You may wish to lay the flowers flat on your workbench top this will help you to keep the design in proportion and the stems cut at the correct length

Follow the steps:

1. Find a nicely shaped flower using this as the central placement.
2. Add more flowers to your design keeping the flower heads and stems straight but slightly angled from the first vertical placement.
3. Add the remaining tall flowers. You may wish to use any singular flowers in this design, some suggestions are:

- Tulips, roses, small disbud chrysanthemums and solid stem poppies.

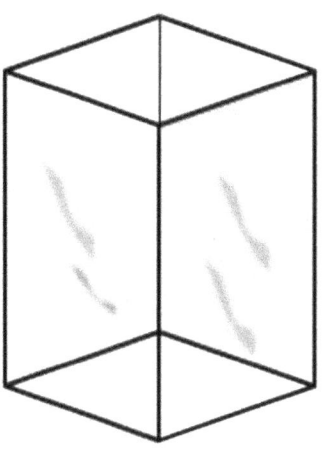

1

2

When you have your larger flowers in the shape you want; you can then add the smaller flowers.

Leave some leaves on the stems.

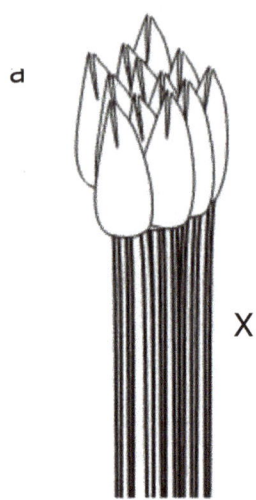

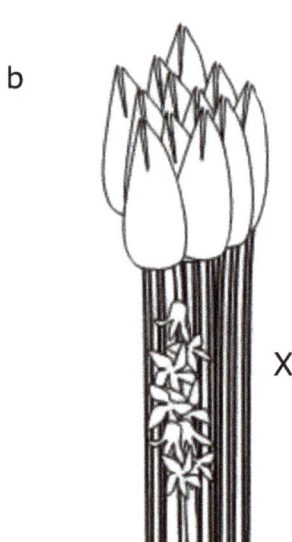

I have added 5 stems of blue hyacinths to the pink tulips.

a. The tulips are in place. Remember, the 'X' in the diagram is the place where all of the stem ends meet.
b. Shows the diagram with 1, hyacinth in place and
c. The finished design with all of the hyacinths added.

modern massed design and goes well in modern homes.

Hot Tip
Many single-stemmed flowers can be used in this modern design, calla lilies look exceptionally striking.

A Variation On A Layered, Two-Colour Flower Arrangement

1

I am using a wide float bowl for this arrangement; however, a glass plate or cake stand will also make a nice display.

Flowers and foliage used in this arrangement:

- 3 stems of yellow Tiger lilies
- 10 yellow roses or 2 stems of white spray chrysanthemums
- A selection of lemons or oranges.

2

I have secured about a $1/8^{th}$ piece of oasis with bowl tape into a small dish – this will help to keep the oasis moist.

Follow the steps:

1. The oasis is secured into the small bowl container.
2. A selection of oranges and lemons are used to make the base of the design. When placing your fruit into its position, make sure the fruit is of similar size and face the fruit in a similar direction.

Once the fruit is in its position, it is time to start arranging your flowers.

3

3. The first placement of a lily stem is inserted into place in the oasis.
4. Keeping the stem as straight and as steady as possible you are now ready for the flower placements 2 and 3. The lily flowers are standing tall and secure. In this arrangement I have left the stamens on the lily flowers, you may wish to gently pull them off – do not cut the stamens from the flower with scissors; this is unsightly and takes most of the natural beauty from the flower.

5. I have made a small posy of roses with a slightly taller flower towards the back this gives a little height to the posy design. When creating this type of arrangement, make sure to keep the two arrangements separate though they form one design.
6. Two large succulent leaves have been inserted into the oasis to give the framework strength and delineation to the overall design.
7. Shows the roses replaced by small posy of white chrysanthemum flowers.

4

5

6

7

Hot Tip
In exceptionally hot climates, replace fresh flowers with fresh foliage but still use fresh fruit if available. Fruit and foliage arrangements create fascinating and interesting designs.

A Traditional, Loose Australian Native Flower Arrangement Using Layered Colours in Fruit

Using fruit in floral arrangements can save money; using fruit has another advantage and that is the use of the intense colour and shape of the fruit when it is combined into your design.

Flowers and foliage used in this arrangement:

- A large bunch of clean gum foliage
- Found native bush foliage
- 3 Banksia flowers and
- Flowering gum foliage
- A selection of available fruit

Again, keep your container simple. If you can, layer your fruit for visual impact.

Follow the steps:

1. Choose a clear glass, plain container.
2. Layer your fruit. Fruit sizes can be a problem when the container is narrow or has shapes within its form. In these arrangements, try to avoid using soft fruits such as plums, peaches, cherries as the weight of the upper fruit can and does easily crush the softer fruit. Cut the oasis to fit snugly into the upper rim of the container. Before securing the oasis, wrap it securely in cling film and place it into position.
3. Insert your foliage into the sides of the oasis keeping these placements strictly as side placements. The top of the oasis is for your flower stem placements.
4. In picture 4, the top surface of the foam is seen and is left free allowing

for easy inserting of your flower stem ends.

5. In picture 5, more flowering native Australian foliage is added. This addition will carry through the visual weight, colour and texture from the gum foliage. The full arrangement is not limited to its impact to maximise the beauty of the Australian bush.
6. Three larger Banksia flowers have been added. Together with these flowers you can see the addition of gum nuts and other larger gum foliage which gives a striking contrast to the overall arrangement. In this picture I have changed the shape of the glass container giving you more ideas of the versatility of such arrangements.
7. Picture seven shows again, a different container creating more interest. The overall arrangement has fruit placed as embellishments outside of the contained fruit within the glass container. When arranging any embellishments to your design, make sure you are adding these to add interest to your work. Embellishments can become so ornate that they can rapidly detract and destroy your design.

Hot Tip
Adding embellishments to your work needs to be done with careful thought and consideration.

Taking A Different Slant On Fruit And Flower Arrangements

A clear glass vase has been chosen for this elegant design. Such creative pieces can be used to decorate at a wedding reception or in a formal setting.

Flowers and foliage used in this arrangement:

- 3 stems of white Tiger lilies
- 10 white roses
- 3 succulent leaves
- 2 stems of flowering prunus blossom
- 2 bags of small mandarins.

Follow the steps:

1. Small mandarins are used to fill this medium sized glass vase.
2. A ¼ block of oasis is measured to snugly fit the vase opening. Once the size of the oasis is correct, the oasis is soaked in water. Larger magnolia (or equivalent) leaves are pinned onto the oasis to secure them. Overlapping the leaves: use 2-4 cut wires for each leaf as you secure them into place. To cut the florist wire to the correct length, please follow the directions: (a through to c).
3. The leaf-covered oasis is seen sitting in the opening of the glass vase. The oasis needs to sit and be secure within the opening of the vase. Please see picture 3. The first placement of a stem of lilies is seen in the picture, please note: as seen, the stem end needs to penetrate the oasis at least 2/3 from the front of the oasis.
The leaf-covered oasis block sits above the mandarins. Prior to covering with leaves, the oasis can be wrapped in cling film, this will help to retain the

1

2

Making Hair Pin Wires to secure each leaf onto the oasis

a) Take on single florist wire: 24 gauge x 9 inch length or .56 x 23, 35, 45 cm length.

b) Cut the wire into 3 or 4 equal lengths

c) Bend each into a hairpin wire shape.

Please note: if florist wires are not available use dressmaking pins, hair pins of something suitable.

3

The hairpin wire is used to secure your leaves onto the oasis. Make sure the leaves are of equal size and the wire pins are secured through the outside,

moisture in the oasis and stops the fruit from becoming damaged.

4. The leafed-up oasis sits snugly in the top of the vase.
5. The first long placement of a lily stem is seen in the picture. The leaves have been removed from most of the stem leaving just a few at the lily head.
6. Two extra lily stems are inserted into the oasis base.
7. A carefully placed green curved, succulent stem, showing a different line and leaf shape, has been inserted into the oasis to the right of the design.
8. The first horizontal placement is inserted to the right side of the oasis. This placement is in direct contrast in visual line of the previous placements. The willowy shapes of prunus blossom add delightful movement to the static contrast of the lily stems.
9. A second placement of the blossom is made to the left of the design. In the same picture, you will see that a group of white roses has been added. The roses are inserted into the oasis, one at a time keeping the tall flower to the back in the first placement. Each flower stem is measured before cutting the stem. This technique allows for vital measurements to be maintained. The roses are kept compact and closely together as they are placed into position, this gives a modern twist to this arrangement. Two large leaves are secured into the oasis. The deep green of the leaves give a different depth of colour and adds a distinctive shape and strength to what is primarily a vertical design. The posy of white roses adds a delightful visual stopping point to this interesting arrangement.
10. To give a definitive visual starting point to the arrangement, a bunch of fresh, green grapes has been added to the focal point.

4 5

6 7

8

9

10

Hot Tip
Do not hesitate to use local fruit and foliages, if available in your flower arrangements.

A Simple Box of Flowers

Boxes of flowers make an ideal present at any time. The box can be a cost effective substitute to buying an expensive vase or container.

Flowers and foliage used in this arrangement:

- 9 pink roses
- 2 Stems of white Tiger lilies
- 4 stems of white spray carnations
- 2 stems of white column stock
- A variety of small-leafed foliage.

Follow the steps:

1. Create your box and line with strong water-resistant cellophane; surround the oasis with a coloured water-resistant paper.
2. Sit ½ block of soaked oasis squarely into the box.
3. Create a base of foliage (not too tall). If you can use a variety of different greens in the colour it will enhance the appearance of your design. Try also to use different shapes and texture in your foliage this also adds 'eye appeal' to your design.
4. The first two placement stem ends of lilies are firmly secured into the oasis base. If it is needed, extra, taller foliage can be added to enhance the backdrop of the design however, care should be taken adding extra foliage once any placements are in place within the oasis. I am relying on the lilies to add the foliage support needed to give the design its base framework. Some shorter pieces of foliage are added to the front placement of the

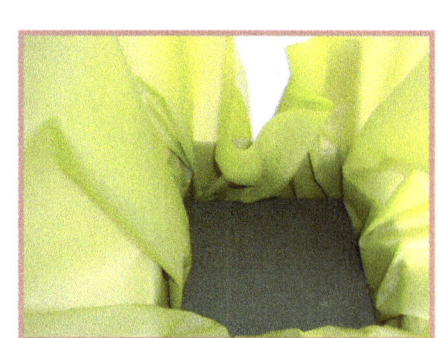

lilies this is adding support for the next flowers to be put into place.

5. Small white spray carnations are added, then the semi-open pink roses. Starting with a taller-stemmed rose to the back of the design and placed closely to the first two lily stems.

Continue to visually measure your flower stems before you cut them. Carefully place each flower into the required space, grading the carnations and rose head sizes and the flower's visual impact within the overall design before cutting the stem.

6. To the left of the arrangement, 2 stems of white, sweet-smelling stock flower stems are secured into the oasis creating this beautiful design.
7. To complete the arrangement: a green ribbon is tied around the box and a nice bow is made to create the finished design. This picture shows a clean and refreshing completed arrangement.

Making A Bow

Choose your ribbon to match your flowers. You will need two pieces of ribbon.
Measure your box circumference; the first piece of ribbon is used to go around the box. This piece needs to be long enough to tie the bow into place.

The bow: Hold the ribbon between your thumb and index finger. Fold the left over the right strands making a figure eight, adjust the proportions as you go.

The Completed Box Flower Arrangement

Hot Tip
Use good quality ribbon; using cheap ribbon could ruin your design.

A Two-Flower Arrangement

Creating arrangements with a limited number of flowers can be an invigorating and beautiful experience. By using limited numbers of flowers, you will need to think differently ('think outside of the box'), this thinking will help you to get your creative juices running; it will extend your creative talent and show you different aspects of what you can achieve.

Flowers and foliage used in this arrangement:

- 2 yellow sunflowers
- Enough wide leafed foliage to pin or insert into a ½ block of oasis
- About 20 stems of spear grass
- Enough Nandina foliage to make a block base within a part of the oasis.

Follow the steps:

1. I have used a brightly coloured red flower pot to create the container for this design. To begin, measure your oasis to the size of your container; soak the oasis until it's saturated through; then secure it into your container. In this picture you can see large leaves have been cut from a bush. Laurel or leaves shaped like laurel leaves are excellent for this type of filling or greening-up of your oasis.
2. The leaves are secured by their stem ends into the oasis. In this picture, you can see the leaves go completely around the circumference of the oasis.
3. I have used spear grass as the first placement; spear grass gives a slender elegant outline to many designs. Other tall straight reed type grasses can also be used in such a placement.
4. Once the spear grass is in position

short-stemmed Nandina foliage is added to give the design difference in colour, shape and texture.

5. Sunflower stems are thick and weighty to put into oasis foam. You can add to the security of the sunflower placements by securing and inserting a wooden skewer into the stem end before placing the stem end into the oasis.
6. The angle of the focal point of the largest sunflower is slightly facing forward; this angle gives a warmth and interest to the design.
7. The completed design is shown with the spear grass creating a cage like appearance over the sunflower placements. To use spear grass in this way:
   a) Put the tallest single spear grass into the oasis at the back of the design; bring the spear grass forward, bending carefully (spear grass snaps easily so care in the bending needs to take place).
   b) Follow the same procedure with each single piece of spear grass you add to your design. Measure, create the void and space you want to have around your flowers, then cut or break the grass to the required length.
   c) In picture 7, I have created an arc effect by curving and measuring, cutting or breaking the spear grass before it is finally fixed into the oasis

Hot Tip
Shinny surfaced containers add a depth of luxury to your design, whereas, rough surfaces can make your design seem hard and masculine.

Pretty In Pinks

Many techniques can be developed to create the flower arrangement you want to make.

When you have a wide rimmed container, to fill the container with oasis would be unsightly, very costly and you would use many more flowers than you need to.

Flowers and foliage used in this arrangement:

- 5 pink disbud chrysanthemums
- 6 plum coloured miniature calla lilies
- 8 deep pink roses
- Long, narrow gum leaves
- A selection of found foliage

On page 27, I have described, through creating hairpin wires, these can be used to attach leaves to the oasis. Again, in this design I am using this same technique.

The container this time is a tall wine glass shape. This shape is both elegant and can be used for a number of different occasions.

Follow the steps:

1. Using ½ of a block of oasis; make sure the oasis is soaked in water before you start to use it.
2. If you wish, wrap the oasis in cling film prior to pinning the leaves into place. Cling film is easy to penetrate even with some softer stems. The leafed-up oasis is shown sitting snugly in a small container.
3. The diagram shows you where to place the first stem placement in the oasis.
4. As you look at the picture, the first placement of the chrysanthemum is

1

2

3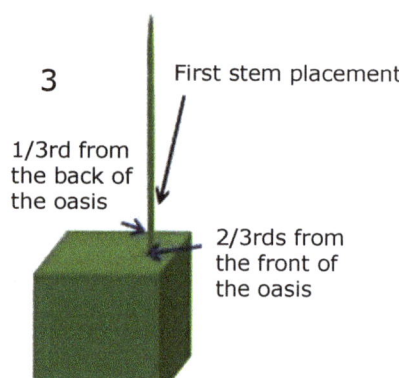

4

5

6

visually measured and placed in the oasis to the right of the oasis; this placement is inserted 2/3rds from the front of the oasis.

5. The second chrysanthemum length is again, visually measured and is placed into the oasis slightly to the left and in front of the first placement.
6. As each placement is made in the oasis, the flower stems and design move slowly forward on the oasis.
7. The fourth chrysanthemum is now cut and put into place. However, this bloom is placed to the right of the third placement. When this type of placement is made, the visual impact of the placements starts to take place. You can see by following the line of the flower heads that a 'C' or crescent shape has emerged in the design.
8. To add more interest to the design 3 mini plum-coloured calla lilies have been placed in the oasis and to the right of the second and third of the placements of chrysanthemums.
9. In picture 9, you can see a further 3 mini calla lilies are put to the left of the chrysanthemums and have been placed lower and at different angles to add interest to the developing design.
10. Strong elegant gum leaves are placed into the oasis to the left of the design with a large green leaf being used as part of the focal point. The smooth surface of the leaves could be classed a feminine textures where as the chrysanthemums are course and masculine in texture.
11. Voids and interest can be created in floral designs by adding different foliage and using it in creative ways. Again, loops of spear grass have been added and placed into the side of the oasis separately. Do not add such feature foliage in great quantities; they must always be used as separate pieces to create features in the design.

12 A second large green leaf is added to the right side of the design. This addition helps to continue the visual balance that allows the arrangement to bring pleasure when it is viewed. To add to the design's impact, 8 deep pink roses have now been placed into the focal area of the design. These roses are placed at different heights allowing the shorter and larger roses to create rhythm, interest and difference.

Once you have an understanding of flower design principles, you can create a wide range of different and exciting creations.

This design has used both colour blocking, different shapes and textures which create different sections of interest within the design. Such a combination of flowers can be put into a vase and be of little of interest but by using skill and technique, these same flowers can also be used to create a striking piece of art.

Hot Tip
As you become more aware of floral design, become bold in the colours, texture, flowers and foliage you use. Each placement then becomes an adventure and the start of a creative journey.

11

12

A Combination Of Three

Using glass candlesticks, roses and pearls; what else can create the visual feeling of celebration and elegance?

Flowers and foliage used in this arrangement:

- 5 dusky pink roses
- 5 deep pink roses
- Red and green Nandina foliage.

Follow the steps:

1. Measure the top of the candlestick circumference, cut your oasis accordingly and soak thoroughly in water prior to use.
2. Three different heights in candlesticks have been chosen to create this stunning three-in-one design.
3. The medium and taller candlesticks have been chosen to create the elegance required. Wispy pieces of Nandina foliage are used as the foliage to cover the oasis.

4. The two arrangements are made together. If you completely make one of a pair at one time, you will find that it is difficult to keep a similarity within the placements. So, when you place a flower in one design, then go and place a flower in the second design. By using this technique you will keep your placements in proportion. The two arrangements are partially made. Each arrangement needs 5 more roses in each to finish both designs.
5. The remaining roses are added to the designs with extra Nandina foliage added as the extra roses are placed into each design.

6. Fine strands of pearls are laid over the flowers. The thread of pearls continues and is shown to catch the corner of the third glass candlestick. Further pearls are carried down onto a round mirror base. Two more candles are added to the design with a pink rose resting of the mirror base. To finish the design, the candles are lit and the ambiance of the moment is captured.

Hot Tip
Roses can last twice as long when they are well conditioned, my **Hot Tip:** fill a deep container: bucket or bath, add two teaspoons of sugar or flower food; cut each stem end diagonally; (this will expose more cell area within the s tem), immediately put the stem ends into deep water up to the rose head letting them float – this technique works wonders for all roses.

How Pretty Are Blue and Pink?

There are a range of containers to use. In the following design, I have used a crystal embellished candle container; this shows the versatility of many containers.

Flowers and foliage used in this arrangement:

- 5 blue iris flowers
- 1 stem of pink Tiger lilies
- A variety of foliage

Follow the steps:

1. A piece of oasis is measured to the size of the small container. The oasis is thoroughly soaked in water prior to making the design. The first placements are 2 iris flowers. The flower stems are visually measured but cut at different lengths, please see the picture. The stem ends are inserted into the oasis. The second placements are the 2 wispy pieces of Nandina foliage placed to the left of the oasis.
2. Two more iris flowers are visually measured against the first two placements; work with the flow of the stem, including and bends or straightness. The curving iris stem pulls the eye back into the centre of the arrangement. The fourth iris placement forms part of the focal point for the overall design.
3. In this picture, lily buds are used as transition materials in their left and right placements. A further fifth open blue iris now forms the focal area within the design.
4. Once the lily buds are in place as described in point 3, 2 large separate leaf stem ends are inserted into the

1

2

3

front of the oasis. The leaves have been wiped clean prior to their use.

5. Some further wispy Nandina is placed to the right side of the oasis. Again, this extends the visual impact of the design. A silver and glass reflection display plate is placed under the arrangement giving a depth of visual transition and interest.

Hot Tip
Iris flowers are shade loving and like cool areas. Equally so, if your flower arrangement is going into a hot venue, your arrangement will lose its lustre very quickly.

4

5

Making Easy Christmas Arrangements

Dried holly leaves have been sprayed gold to help to give these Christmas arrangements a slightly different look. At the time of spaying the holly the 2 terracotta pots were also sprayed gold.

Flowers and foliage used in this arrangement:

- Holly leaves (fresh or artificial)
- 21 oranges in the 3 arrangements (fresh or artificial)
- 6 lemons (fresh or artificial
- Small-leafed, gold painted foliage
- 3 largish Granny Smith apples for the centre arrangement (fresh or artificial)
- 1 stem of white tiger lilies
- 2 stems of white spray carnations

Follow the steps

1. Measure and cut your oasis to the required size. In pictures 1 and 2, I have used dry oasis.
2. Layers of fruit can be secured into many different bases by using wooden skewers. When the fruit is heavy, use 2 skewers for each piece of fruit. Each skewer is pushed into the fruit in different parts; this technique stops the fruit from spinning or the skewer collapsing.
3. The diagram shows how heavy fruit can be secured into the oasis with wooden skewers.
4. Moving on to the next part of the threesome. A variety of garden foliage, picked early in the morning, has been lightly sprayed with the same gold paint that was used to spray the holly and containers. This foliage with its different shapes, forms and textures are placed into wet oasis to form a

cone-shape giving a shape to the initial design.

5. The first placements are brightly coloured oranges. The oranges are a heavy fruit so the method of using 2 wooden skewers is ideal to keep the fruit in place.
6. The next placements are small white spray carnations placed into the centre of the oasis and through the already inserted and placed gold and green foliage. Being a cone shaped design, it is ideal for any Christmas feast, sitting in the middle of the festive table. The solid form of Green Granny Smith apples are ideal to place into the design at this point, again, 2 wooden skewers are used to secure each piece of fruit.
7. Large cream tiger lilies are added to the fruit in the arrangement. The buds are not forgotten, these help to add a different shape and profile which adds interest to the cone shape. Small, skewered mandarins are ideal features in any Christmas arrangement; these can be randomly dotted through your design.
8. The three arrangements are brought together to form the combination of three. Remember, fresh or artificial fruit can be used in these designs. Variations in colour, texture and shape of the materials used all play their role in creating flower arrangements to create ambiance and joyfulness.

Hot Tip
Creating beautiful flower arrangements can be a hobby that gives hours of satisfaction to the flower arranger. Please take the time to enjoy your work and the creations you produce.

6

7

8

A Christmas Treat

As a flower designer you can give yourself a lot of fun with the combinations of materials you use. I must admit, we all, even the professionals, at times get stuck for ideas…!

A stylish silver metal and crystal candlestick is used as the container for the design. A 1/3rd block of oasis has been soaked in water, different shapes in the foliage choice have been cut from the garden, again and as in the previous Christmas arrangement on page 41, the foliage is sprayed with gold paint. To make a different design, use the unobvious materials to create interest, fun and excitement.

Flowers and foliage used in this arrangement:

- 5 sunflowers
- Green and gold small-leafed foliage
- 9 bright orange mandarins

Follow the steps:

1. In this picture, the candlestick is shown with the soaked oasis in place.
2. Short stems of the sprayed gold foliage are inserted into the sides of the oasis.
3. Extra pieces of foliage are placed to the top and at angles to give a nice cushion shape to the design.
4. The first flower placement is a bright yellow sunflower; once visually measured, a skewer is inserted into the stem end and gently moved into the flower head.
5. More sunflowers are placed into the oasis giving a rounded appearance. (Remember to visually measure each stem before you cut it ready for its placement. Accuracy and patience

with cutting your stem ends precisely will save you money, frustration and stress.)

6 The arrangement with the mandarins in place. These are secured with the two-pronged skewer technique mentioned on page 41.

7 The completed design. Adding elegance and interest, a second, shorter container containing mandarins is placed on a mirror, reflective base. A lighted candle adds to the atmosphere and stylishness of the combination of the design its embellishments.

Hot Tip
Sun flowers will hang their heads when there is not enough water getting to the flower head. To well condition flowers when using them in this type of arrangement: cut off as much stem as possible, soak the stem end (up to the head), then arrange them in your design. The difference to their appearance is remarkable: they will show a clarity of petal structure and freshness that will last for days.

Published by Books For Reading On Line.com .,
under licence from MSI Ltd, Australia
Company Registration No: 96963518255
NSW, Australia

This book forms part of the CPD Accredited Course for Fast Track Commercial Floristry Course

See our website: www.how-to-books.com & www.booksforreadingonline.com

Or contact by email: sales@booksforreadingonline.com or: admin@booksforreadingonline.com
Front & Back Covers and Copyright owned by MSI, Australia

MSI acknowledges the author of the images used in this book.

Photography by Christine Thompson-Wells ©
How-To-Books.com is a subsidiary of Books For Reading On Line.com